St. Mary's Church today

ST. MARY'S CHURCH TERRIER

1601

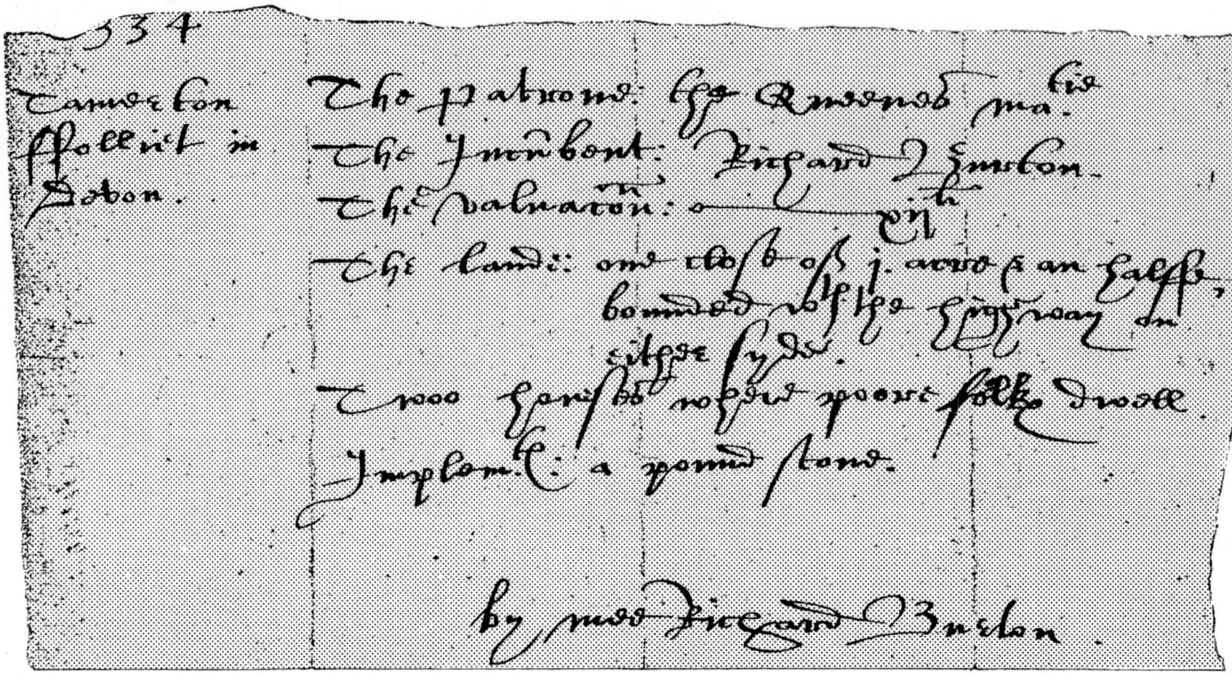

TRANSCRIPTION OF THE ABOVE

Tamerton
ffolliet in
Devon

The patrone:	the Queenes majestie
The incumbent:	Richard Burton
The valuation:	£12
The land:	one close of one acre and a halfe, bounded with the highway on either syde.

Twoo howses where poore folkes dwell.

Implementes:	a pound stone.

by mee Richard Burton

(The original is held in the Devon Record Office, at Exeter.)

SAINT MARY'S CHURCH

TAMERTON FOLIOT

We do not know when the first local church was built but the evidence suggests that there has been Christian worship here at least since 900 AD, and possibly much longer.

Before leaving Britain about the middle of the fifth century the Romans had been in the west country and left some traces east of the river Plym[1] but no visible signs of their occupation along the river Tamar, although it has been suggested that they may have had a lookout post on Warleigh Tor. Although the Romans introduced Christianity to this country, no-one has recorded whether they tried to convert the heathen Britons in the south west. During the centuries after their departure the land was controlled first by the Angles and later by the Saxons, and during this period Celtic missionaries came from Ireland into Cornwall and Devon and beyond; as a result the West Saxon royal house was converted, and one of its members (Aldhelm) became Abbot of Glastonbury.[2]

At first these visiting monks were concerned with establishing rallying-points for those whom they had converted, usually marked by the setting-up of a cross in wood or stone to which they brought a small portable altar. When such a spot had been regularly used for some time, a small chapel (or sanctuary) was erected to protect the altar from the weather; the faithful were left exposed to the elements until such time as they decided to build themselves a shelter by constructing what we would now call the nave of a church.[3]

It is recorded that two such missionaries who came to this area in the seventh century were Saint Indract and Saint Dominic.[4] The historian Wiliam of Malmesbury, writing early in the 12th century has an interesting story to tell about them:

"Indractus, son of a certain king in Ireland, being of an upright life, decided to spurn the pleasures of the king's court and go on a pilgrimage to Rome. With nine companions and his sister Dominica, he set out on the voyage, calling at Britain on the way, where they landed at a port called Tamerunta and lived there a most strict life in the service of God for a long time, and built an oratory in which to pray. And in that place Indract fixed his pilgrim's staff in the ground, and straightway in the sight of all it brought forth roots, boughs and leaves, and in course of time grew into a huge and shady oak . . . Fearing that a longer stay would not be pleasing to God, he and his companions hastened on to Rome . . . Returning afterwards to Britain he determined to go to Glastonbury to the shrine of St. Patrick, and whilst there he was murdered."

One can only conjecture about the truth of this story, but there is strong support for the view that Tamerunta is Tamerton Foliot, and that the two Saints sailed up the creek and landed here about the year 689 AD.[5] Indract may indeed have founded our first village church and this could possibly have been dedicated to his name, but he does not appear in any ecclesiastical calendar today although down to the 13th century St. Indract's Day was apparently celebrated on the 8th May.[6] Another Saint, St. Budoc, also landed in Tamerton creek, and founded a church at Budoc's hide (Budshead) but the building has long since disappeared.

The Saxons did much to unify England and to provide it with an orderly system of government. For this purpose they divided the country into counties and into hundreds, and also set up an early parish system, the king giving land to any of his men who would go and settle there. Among these settlers, those who were already converted to Christianity would build a church or chapel beside their house and their estate would then become the parish.[7]

The Saxons were not skilled in working with stone and most of their churches were built of wood, so that very few have survived. There is no trace today of any Saxon building in Tamerton, although it is fairly certain that a church or chapel of some kind existed here,[8] and the site of the present church seems its most likely location — on a patch of rising ground, close to a settlement of people and communication routes, not far from the head of the creek. It is probable that the residence of the local thegn (lord) was close by, and the priest may have acted as his chaplain.[9]

The Viking invasions of Britain in the 10th century resulted in the destruction of many church buildings, especially monasteries, and they came dangerously close to Tamerton when they sacked Tavistock Abbey, but there is no evidence of them actually coming here.

A number of Saxon churches were erected in Devon well before the Norman Conquest but all of them that survived were rebuilt later in more permanent materials. The Domesday Survey (1086) does not always list them, and it contains no mention of any church at Tamerton Foliot. This is strange since from the detail quoted in the Survey it is clear that by 1086 there was already an established population here and cultivated settlement.[10] The first record of a church building, presumably a Norman structure, occurs in a letter dated 1186 from the Bishop of Exeter to the Prior and Convent of Plimton, confirming the grants which had been made by earlier Bishops of land and tithes relating to the church of Tamerton Foliot.[11] Structural evidence which survived until the 19th century suggested that the early church was a small rectangular building about the size of a chapel, with two square-headed windows in its north and south walls, located at the east end of the present north aisle; additional support for this view is given by the existence there of the Gorges tomb (1350) as well as most of the memorials to later lords of the manor.

The Exeter Episcopal Registers show that in 1279 the Bishop committed the custody of the Tamerton Vicarage to Sir Richard le Deneis, chaplain. The church at Tamerton is listed, together with the chapel at Martinstowe (Maristow) in a papal valuation of church property made in 1288.[12]

By the 12th century the Exeter diocese was one of the largest and richest in the country, with a well-organised parish system. A lot of new church building was occurring, much of it done by local landowners for the use of their dependents and tenants.[13] The church at Tamerton Foliot must have been in process of being altered in 1292, since in that year the Pope granted a remission of punishment for sins committed "to all who with true penitence visit the Church of St. Mary of Tamerton Foliot on the feasts of Blessed Mary and St. Denis",[14] and in 1318 the Bishop dedicated the high altar and three other altars in this church.[15]

A change in roof-levels (which remained until the 19th century) showed clearly how the 13th century building had been enlarged by more than doubling its length, an internal arch at the point of junction marking the difference in height. The extension was lighted by two pointed windows, and an entrance door provided near the west end of the north wall; this doorway was still clearly visible, although blocked up, until the rebuilding at the end of the 19th century. The roof was almost certainly thatched, and it is probable that there was a bell-turret at the west end.[16] This is how the church might have appeared from Church Row lane about 1350:—

During the 14th and 15th centuries there was a big increase in population in the county, and many churches were extended or rebuilt, usually in the style called Perpendicular.[17] By then Tamerton Foliot church appears to have been in need of further enlargement, and about 1440 this was done by the addition of a wide nave and a new chancel. The south wall of the original church was taken down and replaced by a row of granite pillars and arches; curiously, some of the capitals on these pillars were cut from the softer moorstone. The roof over the new chancel was built lower than that over the nave,[18] matching the two different roof-levels of the original building; this may explain why the two arches at the eastern end are rounded whilst the rest are pointed. The tower which is 78 feet high appears to have been put up at the same time as the nave, providing a home for four bells and possibly also serving as a lookout as well as providing an external feature of distinction. Perhaps the faces on the gargoyles are those of the masons who built it, looking pleased at being near the end of their task.

At this stage the building must have appeared to be rather lop-sided, with its original structure now forming the north aisle. The south aisle, which was added about 1500, was made five feet wider than the north aisle,[19] and included a south entrance porch; its later date of construction was revealed through the shape of its windows, which were made in the Late Perpendicular style. Instead of granite, Roborough stone (moorstone) was used for the pillars and arches separating the nave from the south aisle, the pillar-capitals being cut to a slightly different shape from those on the north side of the nave.

Whilst the growth in population during the Middle Ages had often necessitated churches being enlarged, it also created over-crowding in the towns which facilitated the spread of disease. The Black Death reached England from the Continent thirty years after the dedication of the altars in St. Mary's Church; its effects were particularly serious in the Exeter diocese, and nearly half the clergy died.[20] Despite the relative isolation of Tamerton Foliot it is unlikely that the village escaped the disease entirely, and it is not surprising to find that there was a succession of four vicars between 1349 and 1351. Whether any of the first three died from the plague is not recorded.

Perhaps due to the very poor road surfaces, possibly encouraged too by fears about disease, many of the larger houses in the county had their own private chapel.[21] Warleigh House had one which was first licensed by the Bishop about 1250; the chapel of St. Martin at Blaxton (later incorporated into Maristow House) existed well before that date. Tamerton Foliot was a large parish about six and a half square miles in extent, and its roads were not always in good repair; in 1410 Bishop Stafford, possibly thinking about his episcopal visitations, provided money for the repair of the bridges and also the road between Plymouth and Tamerton Foliot.[22]

It was common at the time to make payments to the church for masses to be sung and prayers said to assist the faithful, whether living or dead. Richer families would endow a Chantry for this purpose, and this would normally be associated with a particular altar in the church. Such a Chantry was endowed in Tamerton church early in the 16th century;[23] the entry in the Chantry Rolls reads as follows:—

> "*Tamerton Folyett.*
> *The chauntrye there. Founded by John Copleston Esqur. To fynde a pryste to praye for hym and the sowles of his parents and other his frynds in the parysh church of Tamerton Folyett. And he to have a pencon of £6 yerely going owt of the lands and tenements in Warleghe and Tamerton Folyett belonging to the heires of the sayd Copleston.*"

The Chantry was most probably located in the north aisle, perhaps where the Copleston family monument is now erected, but it was not to survive very long.

The Reformation, and Henry VIII's break with the Pope in 1529, resulted in great changes in religious life in England, although it was several years before these changes reached south west Devon.[24] The immediate result of the Dissolution of the Monasteries after 1536 was to transfer the patronage of Tamerton Foliot church (i.e. the right to appoint the Vicar) from the Convent at Plympton to the King. Some years after this all Chantry Chapels were suppressed. A different form of service was introduced and a new Prayer Book. There was a wave of reaction against many of the old, long-established practices and beliefs.

Tamerton Foliot Church about 1900
(note the narrow north aisle and the two roof levels.)

Interior of the church in 1830

This movement continued after Edward VI succeeded to the throne. He appointed Commissioners for each region of the country and instructed them to make an Inventory of Church Goods for every church in their region. All 'popish images' were then to be removed. As a result carved roods and crucifixes were destroyed, vestments burned, valuable church plate melted down and sold, and medieval ornaments including stained glass windows and carved screens often smashed.[25] Church bells however were apparently exempt from this edict, and the Commissioners Inventory dated 1553 records that "Tamerton Folyett has 4 bells in the tower there", and the churchwardens were charged to keep them "unspoiled, unembesiled and unsold". Four was a large number of bells at that time for a church in this district, none of its near neighbours having more than three.[26]

After the death of Edward VI, Mary sought to restore the mass and the authority of the Pope, and she stopped further destruction of the artistic treasures of the medieval church, but by then it was almost too late. Much had already gone, although in some parishes the people had hidden material away and were able to bring it out again. If anything was so preserved at Tamerton, it has since disappeared. When Elizabeth I was made Head of the English Church, she forbade celebration of the mass, and the clergy had to accept the 39 Articles of Religion in which the doctrine of the Church was laid down. Laymen were expected to attend church regularly, or in default to pay a fine.[27]

Some west Devon parishes rebelled strongly against the loss of the Roman mass and its liturgical associations, but Tamerton apparently accepted Protestantism more willingly. St. Mary's Church lost its rood screen and its eucharistic vestments, and there is no evidence that it retained any of the former Catholic imagery. For over two hundred years subsequently its walls remained plain and white-washed, and even as late as 1850 it possessed no stained glass windows and no cross on its communion table. "There was merely a biblical inscription, painted in insipid colours, on the wall on either side of the east window".[28] At about the same time the churchyard was described as "very pretty, rural and retired".[29]

The period of Cromwell and the Commonwealth (1649-1660) brought an even sterner wave of puritanism. In the rural Devon parishes a large number of clergy were turned out of their livings, and replaced by 'Ministers' more acceptable to the authorities. Later on, when Charles II succeeded to the throne this process was reversed, which must have left everybody in a state of confusion. Here at Tamerton William Baylie was replaced by Minister Robert Wyne, and he in turn was replaced by Alexander Fitzgeffry who was presumably more acceptable in the changed times. A number of the Puritan Ministers who were thus rejected by the Established Church subsequently set up their own religious meetings, so laying the foundations of Non-conformity.[30]

Puritanism placed great emphasis on preaching, and the pulpit replaced the altar as the focal point in the church. From about the 14th century there had been some preaching to the people in their own language, for which the congregation usually stood around the pulpit. Apart from an occasional bench no seats were provided, and it was not until the 16th century that even the lord of the manor had his own pew.[31] By 1700 however "family pews" were commonplace for those who could afford to rent them, and by then Tamerton Foliot church was filled with a number of high-sided pews of various sizes, each allotted to a family or house, the larger ones having seats around them on three sides so that some were seated facing the back of the church.

The Jacobean carved pulpit stood high up on a pedestal, near the east end of the nave in front of the communion table. From his elevated position the preacher could see which pews were occupied and which were not — important, since the Act of Uniformity of 1552 had imposed a duty on all persons to attend divine service on every Sunday and Holy Day unless they had a lawful or reasonable excuse to be absent. The sermons were usually long and not always easy to follow, so it is not surprising to find the churchwardens paying a man to keep the boys quiet at the back of the church;[32] nor to read that the high-sided pews were thought to be "conducive to irreverence and sin".

As the population continued to grow this increased the need for more seating in churches, particularly free seats for the poor who could not afford a pew rent. A number of churches attempted to solve this by building galleries, and these became a common feature in the late 18th century. It was not until 1811 however that a wooden gallery was added to the back of the south aisle in Tamerton church,[33] and this appears to have been used to accommodate the boys from Mary Dean's Charity School. Some years later it was extended across the west end of the nave, in front of the tower, to provide a place for the choir whose members with the musicians had previously been seated on the floor below.

When the Archdeacon visited St. Mary's Church in 1825 he was very critical about the disproportionate amount of space taken up by the rented family pews which resulted in insufficient seating for others. He told the churchwardens bluntly that they should either enlarge the church or erect additional galleries. They did neither.

Ten years later the Rural Dean made similar criticisms, and also suggested that the "high and unsightly" pews should be lowered. It was another fifteen years however before the Church Vestry Committee came up with a specific proposal, and even then the old pews were not replaced until 1852 with the seats that are still there today.

Music in the 17th and 18th century village churches was usually fairly sinple. The Commonwealth Parliament had ordered the abolition of "all superstitious monuments in churches, including organs".[34] we do not know whether Tamerton Foliot church possessed an organ at the time of that order (1644), but it certainly did not have one subsequently before the year 1846 when a harmonium was obtained, although in 1822 the wardens had paid a man £3.8s 0d (£3.40p) for painting and fixing a "sham organ" to the Singing Gallery. For many years music in the church had been provided by a small orchestra consisting of "a base viol and other instruments", that is to say, a cello and one or two violins probably with a wind instrument such as the serpent (an early form of bassoon). The choir included both men and boys, and was led by the clerk who was provided with a pitch pipe to give them the note.[35] Surviving church accounts for the 18th century include regular expenses for new strings for the orchestra, also candles for the choir as well as an annual payment of £6 for teaching the singers. After the harmonium was installed and an organist appointed the church records make no further reference to the orchestral players who had presumably been disbanded. A pipe organ was not provided until 1895.

After the year 1550 the external appearance of the church here remained unchanged for about 300 years. Repairs obviously had to be done; no building lasts for ever without maintenance. The stone work especially on the tower needed to be pointed regularly, the pinnacles and the weather-vanes repaired. The wooden lattices on the tower windows rotted and had to be replaced so as to keep out the birds, especially the choughs (jackdaws). Children playing in the churchyard frequently broke the church windows. There was also the problem of damp, due partly to defects in the roof and partly to the level of the soil against the outside walls. The church floor was about two feet lower than the path outside, so that water may have flooded in after heavy rain.

Starting in 1823 the Rural Dean made an annual written report on the state of the building and the churchyard. One of his earliest recommendations was that the earth should be dug away from the outside of the church walls to a depth of four feet, and that the trench so excavated should be paved. He was also concerned about the appearance of the walls inside the church, regularly asking for them to be freshly white-washed, perhaps to obliterate the signs of damp and also smoke-stains from the two coal-burning stoves used to keep the place warm for the services in the winter months. He also wanted the gates and fences to the churchyard to be made high enough to keep out not only straying cattle and pigs, but also "to exclude the public at all times but those of Divine Service",[36] an order which sounds particularly strange today.

By the middle of the 19th century major repairs became necessary to the south aisle, for the restoration of which nearly £700 had to be raised,[37] a considerable amount in 1851 when the work was done. The south porch and the walls of the south aisle were rebuilt; the two galleries at the back of the church were taken down and replaced by a fresh one at the rear of the nave.[38] Window lights were inserted in the slating of the nave roof. The floor of the church was raised about two feet, covering the bottom of the pillars, although the floor of the tower was left at the original level. The old high pews were taken out and replaced by smaller, lower ones,[39] in which the majority of the seats faced the altar. The pulpit was moved to the north side of the nave, adjacent to a pillar. The chancel window was also in need of repair, but this created something of a problem since the chancel was the property (and hence the responsibility) of the lay rector, who at that time seemed to have very little connection with the parish apart from his entitlement to collect income from the Great Tithes. After a great deal of argument about the extent of the work considered essential, and how much the lay rector should contribute to its cost, a settlement was finally reached and the work carried out.[40]

Some years later cracks appeared in the north aisle. It is a remarkable tribute to the original builders that this aisle had been standing, very little changed, for more than five hundred years. Whether due to wear and tear, or perhaps to dislodgment during the work on the chancel, two of the arches in the north aisle began to sag, particularly at the point where the roof changed in height. The deterioration must have occurred slowly, because although it was first noticed in 1865,[41] it was not until thirty years later that a major restoration was undertaken following violent winter storms in 1888 and 1891; in the latter year two large trees crashed on to the roof of the aisle necessitating considerable repair.[42]

The vicar and the churchwardens wanted to widen the north aisle to the same size as the south aisle so as to increase the seating capacity. The lord of the manor opposed widening on the grounds that it would destroy the aisle's architectural features, but after persuasion by the Archdeacon he agreed, suggesting as a compromise that "the aisle be widened and roofed on two levels, as at present".[43] Starting in 1894 the north aisle was pulled down and completely rebuilt the same width as the south aisle. The whole of its roof however was raised to the same level. Regrettably the architect made no attempt to match the exterior appearance of the aisle to that of the rest of the church; dressed limestone blocks were used instead of local stone, and a smaller east window was inserted than its counterpart in the south aisle. In the process of this rebuilding the old north doorway disappeared, as did traces of an early rood screen,[44] so that nothing remained of the 13th century building. The total cost of this restoration was nearly £2,000, and a pipe organ installed at the same time cost an additional £344. It says a great deal for the efforts of everyone concerned (and perhaps also about the increasing wealth in the parish) that both amounts had been paid off by 1900.[45]

For some unexplained reason (perhaps to save expense) the pews in the restored north aisle were re-erected several inches lower than those in the rest of the church, the wooden floor-boards being omitted.

Since 1850 there have been many changes in the furnishings of the church, a reflection of new attitudes both in the parish and in the Church of England generally. Thus a number of changes were made[46] at the west end in 1888, thanks to a generous donation from Sir Massey Lopes (great grandfather of Lord Roborough) which enabled them to remove the west gallery, and also to erect a carved screen at the tower entrance. At the same time the font was transferred from the back of the nave to a Baptistry area at the rear of the south aisle.

The church inventory of 1727, referring to the tower, states: "there was formerly a clock, not maintained by the whole parish, but by part". This clock must either have been repaired or replaced, because for many years subsequently regular payments were made "for winding up the clock in the tower"[47] and in 1849 a striking mechanism was added.[48] Perhaps the sundial over the south entrance door is an indication that the old clock in the tower was not too reliable. At all events, in 1897 the Grigg family of Cann House presented a new clock with a chiming mechanism, and this is still in use; it is a pity that one of its faces was not directed towards the north, since the majority of the people in the village live on that side of the church.

At the time that the north aisle was rebuilt (1894-5) a new altar table and choir stalls were given,[49] so that the choir could now be located in the chancel. Twentieth century changes include panelling of the sanctuary, the furnishing of a side chapel in the north aisle, the installation of both electric power and central heating, the provision of a wooden floor in the tower for the ringers, creating a space underneath for use as a choir vestry, and also the addition of a glass screen to the ringers' chamber. There was a proposal in 1911 to re-seat the church with oak pews,[50] but this came to nothing.

The stained glass windows are relatively modern, the oldest being the east window which was inserted in 1868 in memory of Walter Radcliffe who died in the previous year. Two other stained glass windows on the south wall and three on the west wall, have all been erected as memorials to former parishioners.

The church roof was completely re-slated in 1977, and new guttering provided in 1981. Three months later fire destroyed the roof of the nave and much of the roof of the north aisle; although many of the wooden ribs were badly scorched the roof bosses escaped serious injury, and the south aisle survived unscathed.

The parish stocks now lie in the south porch; there are also two stones, one an ornamented octagonal stone which may possibly formerly have been used as the base of a font; the other is a rectangular piece about 18 inches by 12, with an incised cross on one face.

By mutual consent between the clergy concerned Saltimore (in the parish of Ernesettle) is now in the pastoral care of Tamerton Foliot's vicar, whilst Maristow is in the pastoral care of the vicar of Bickleigh.

The Vicarage and the Glebe

The earliest reference to a Vicarage here is in the Diocesan records, which state that in 1279 the Bishop committed the custody of the Vicarage of Tamerton Foliot to Sir Richard le Deneis, chaplain.[51] At that time it was very poorly endowed, the Taxation Return of Pope Nicholas in 1291 quoting its value as £4 0s 0d including the chapel at Martinstowe (Maristow).[52] But by 1535 the value of the living had risen to £10, and the chapel of Martinstowe was given as 13s 4d.[53]

On 16 July 1600 a certain Richard Retoricke wrote to Mr. William Bruton at Exeter, asking him to search the Dean and Chapter's records for the "composition of the Vicarage of Tamerton Foliot";[54] there is no further evidence of what particular information he sought, nor of any reply being sent. Perhaps he was a churchwarden and wanted to discover if there was a Glebe Terrier in existence; this is a document prepared from time to time to provide an inventory of the church and vicarage as well as the glebe land. The following year such a document was written out, and signed by Richard Burton the Vicar at the time. This, the oldest surviving Glebe Terrier for St. Mary's Church, dated 1601, is a very brief statement, not even mentioning a Vicarage.[55]

In 1613 however, Burton produced another Terrier which reads as follows:

There belongs to the Church of Tamerton aforesaid a vicaradge house with other dwelling houses appertaining thereto an orchard, gardens and a hopyerd, a pound and poundhouse all counted within itself, and one close of land called the sanctuary close lying upon the east syde of the town of Tamerton aforesaid compassed about on both sydes with the highway, and joyning upon part of the bargaine and tenement called Hesende neere to the Church Town of Tamerton aforesaid.

The next Terrier, dated 1680, tells us rather more:

The Vicarage is built with stone and covered with Helling stone. It contains four upper chambers, a parlour, hall, kitching and buttery, all in good and sufficient repayre, two outhouses, one barne, one pound house built partly with stone, partly with earth, covered with thetch.

The plan of this house still exists, and shows how closely it resembled the typical Dartmoor house.[56] Presumably the pound was for keeping in animals which strayed at the time of the village fairs, for which the sheep pens were set up along the Vicarage wall. There was also a village pound at Pound Corner, near the bottom of Fore Street.[57]

By 1745 the glebe land was stated to consist of one orchard, one herb-garden and a little hopyard, also one field of arable land, three acres in all, enclosed with earth hedges. On the churchyard ten trees value five pounds ten shillings, but none on the glebe.

In 1775 the Reverend Coplestone Radcliffe who was then the Vicar, wrote to the Bishop of Exeter to tell him that the Tamerton Vicarage house was in too dilapidated a state to be habitable, part of it being underground and consequently damp; several of the room floors, he said, were so decayed as to need relaying; the walls were unplastered and the upstairs rooms lacked ceilings. In due course the Bishop gave his consent to the building of a new Vicarage, to be sited on the glebe about twenty yards away from the original one. This new house was to be completed within eighteen months.[58] Part of the earlier house was retained and made into a stable, which survived until it was finally pulled down early in the twentieth century.

The new Vicarage can only have been occupied by Mr. Radcliffe for a few years, since in 1782 he accepted the Rectorship of Stoke Climsland, although he continued to hold the living of Tamerton Foliot and paid a Curate to look after its affairs. For over twenty years a succession of Curates lived in Tamerton Vicarage, until the death of Mr. Radcliffe. In 1806 the Reverend Robert Spranger was appointed as the new Vicar and came to live in the Vicarage.

It is a tribute to its builders that this Vicarage house is still in use today after 200 years. An extension was added last century, bringing the building to the edge of the road, and it has since been modernised within, also connected to the main drainage and provided with a new roof. It is not surprising however that the Diocese now wishes to replace it with a newer building which should be less costly to maintain.

Rector and Vicar also the Impropriate (Lay) Rector

Originally the incumbent of the local church was called the Rector, and he had full right to all the church income from tithes arising in the parish. But during the Middle Ages many rectories were appropriated by monastic houses — at Tamerton one of the Foliots gave the church and glebe to the Convent of St. Peter and St. Paul at Plympton. The monastic house then took over the rectorial revenue, and also the advowson whereby they were entitled to nominate a priest (often a monk) who was given the title of Vicar and responsibility for saying the offices and looking after the parish. Henry IV signed a Statute to make the Vicar's position permanent, so that he could no longer be removed at the will of the appropriators, nor could he any longer remain a member of a monastic order and he had to be provided with an income. This normally meant that he was endowed with part of the glebe or church land, and also a share of the parish tithes, namely the "small tithe", the monastic house appropriator retaining the "great tithe". These are sometimes referred to as the "tithe of hay" and the "tithe of corn".

The tithe was a tax of one-tenth of the annual proceeds of land held, originally payable in kind (although later converted into a cash payment) taken for the support of the clergy and the church. Not all livings were appropriated, and in this case the incumbent continued to be called the Rector and retained the entire income from the tithes.

On the Dissolution of the Monasteries (1536-1540) the King took over the monastic appropriations; subsequently many of them were transferred to lay people in return for a service to the sovereign, thus creating Impropriate (Lay) Rectorships, with the same rights to the "great tithe" as the monastery had formerly held. This happened at Tamerton Foliot, although here the Crown reserved to itself the advowson or patronage (the right to appoint the Vicar). Such Impropriate (Lay) Rectorship was a valuable heritable property, and could be sold to new owners. At Tamerton it was first granted by Elizabeth I in 1583, and subsequently changed hands several times, usually by purchase, until the rights were finally extinguished by the Act of 1936 which eliminated tithes. The Impropriate (Lay) Rectorship here was never held by a Lord of the Manor.

These lay persons were quite distinct from the Vicar who continued to be responsible for the spiritual care of the parishioners. The Impropriate (Lay) Rector was usually held responsible for the repair and maintenance of the Chancel, this part of the church being regarded as his or her property, whilst the parish was responsible for the fabric of the rest of the building.

With the abolition of the tithes there is now no practical difference between a Rector and a Vicar.

It is interesting to note that there have been more Vicars of this parish during the 20th century than in any previous one.

List of Vicars of the Parish since 1279 AD
(There was a Church here before this date)

Edward I	Sir Richard le Deneis		1279
	Roger de Sutton	10 March	1283-4
	John le Fleur (Flur)	13 June	1309
Edward II	Nicholas de la Lake		1324
Edward III	John Lingham	24 February	1348-9
	Roger de Harston		1349
	Sir William Mona	5 July	1351
	Sir John Freme	25 August	1351
Richard II	Simon Nywenham		1375
Henry IV	Thomas Baker (Meone)	8 November	1399
Henry V	Thomas Fforde		1413
Henry VI	Ralph Andrew		1443
	Edward Man		1452
	John Carpenter		
Henry VIII	Cornelius Veysey		1517
	John Chubbe		1518
	Richard Cosseyn	18 February	1533-4
	Richard Curtois	June	1546
	John Wiat	September	1546
After this the patronage passed from the Convent at Plympton to the Crown.			
Elizabeth I	Simon Downe		1562
	William Hunt		1566-7
	Nicholas Brusie		1573
	Richard Burton		
James I	Lewis Land		1619
Charles I	William Baylie		1640
	Robert Wyne, Minister		
Charles II	Robert Wyne, Vicar		1660
	Alexander Fitzgeffry		1663
Anne	John Stokes		1706
George II	William Jope		1733
George III	Coplestone Radcliffe		1774
	Robert Spranger		1806
George IV	George Hawker	15 January	1821
	Charles Gower Boyles	25 August	1821
	John Rayner		1827
William IV	Warwick Young Churchill Hunt	29 January	1830
	George Frederick Arthur	23 June	1830
Victoria	Edward Roberts		1871
Edward VII	Stanley Forster-Brown		1910
George V	Cecil R. Martyn		1913
	Oswald W. C. de Blogue		1919
	John B. King		1922
	Bertram H. Meeres		1927
	William Hugh Wood		1928
	Francis B. Soady		1932
George VI	Hubert Spencer		1946
Elizabeth II	William D. Stenhouse		1953
	Michael T. Fermer		1959
	Archibald R. Leggate		1963
	Christopher William Hedley Goodwins		1969

Stone effigies on the altar-tomb in Tamerton Foliot Church

These fine effigies, six centuries old and still in a good state of preservation, show the device of the Gorges family, three gorges or whirlpools one inside the other, on the knight's surcoat. He wears a handsomely fringed and embroidered skirt; his lady wears an attractive head-dress, which is quilted and interlaced with rows of pearls. Both knight and lady have their heads protected by angels. Mutilation of the heads of two of the angels and one animal most probably occurred during the 17th century vandalism of church monuments.

Originally believed to be Sir Ralph de Gorges and his wife Ellen, it is now considered more likely that the figures are those of William de Gorges and his wife Agnes, date about 1346. The drawing is taken from "Ancient Sepulchral Effigies and Monumental Sculpture of Devon" by W. Hamilton Rogers.

Monuments and Memorials

The church is well-endowed with wall-plaques and other memorials which provide links with its past and occasional snatches of rather dubious poetry. The monuments associated with the various lords of the manor are mainly concentrated in the north aisle on what is thought to be the site of the original building.

The memorial to the Foliots is undoubtedly their name, which gives the parish and village a unique and distinct title, as well as opportunity for a variety of spellings! It was long believed that Gilbert Foliot, who became Bishop of London at the time of Archbishop Thomas a Beckett, was a native of Tamerton Foliot. Recent research has shown that he did not come from here, but from a different branch of the Foliot family related to the Earls of Hereford and living in the Gloucester area.[59]

Through the marriage of Ellen Foliot the manors of Warleigh and Tamerton passed to the de Gorges family, one of whose descendants, William de Gorges and his wife are commemorated by a stone altar tomb now situated near the east end of the north aisle. The date of this tomb is thought to be about 1346 or soon after, and it is the earliest monument in the church. Full-length effigies of the knight in armour and his wife lie on the tomb, each with a dog at the feet. It will originally have been identified by a painted coat of arms, which has long since faded or peeled off; it was not the custom until after 1400 to inscribe the name upon a tomb, and there is no sign of any inscription on this one. For a long time it was coated thickly with whitewash. Presumably the bones lie in a vault somewhere beneath the floor, but the tomb itself has been moved at least twice; for a while last century it lay closer to the position of the altar in the side chapel, but was moved back in 1914.

By the marriage of Leva Gorges to Thomas Bonville about 1435, the ownership of the manors passed to a new family whose members have no memorial in the church. The Bonvilles were much involved in State affairs, and had residences in both Devon and Cornwall, and may only have visited Warleigh occasionally. They became the great rivals of the Courtenays (later Earls of Devon), but the Bonville line was extinguished by losses during the Wars of the Roses, and the ownership of the manors passed through Anne Bonville to her husband Philip Copleston.

The most striking monument in the church is the one in memory of John Copleston and his wife Susannah and their family, on the north wall of the north aisle. Erected in 1617, it is now believed to be in its original location, although it has been suggested that it was taken down and hidden away during the period of the Commonwealth to escape being smashed; by 1840 however it was certainly back in position, but it had to be removed to the Warleigh Room during the rebuilding of the aisle in 1894, and damage to the figures was very skilfully repaired by an Exeter craftsman before its re-erection.[60] It illustrates the husband and wife kneeling, facing each other, and underneath are their ten children kneeling similarly. One son and one daughter died in childhood and so carry a skull; one boy carries no sword and he may have died before the age of 14. John is buried in the family vault close by, as is his wife Susannah. She made a second marriage, to Sir Anthony Rous, and her death in 1633 is recorded on a floor-stone.

The Copleston family enjoyed eminence in the county for a long period between the 15th and 17th centuries and the coats of arms depicted on the memorial are of some of the great west country families to whom they were related. An old Devonshire couplet about the families of "Crocker, Cruwys and Copleston" suggests that they were descended from pre-Conquest Devon ancestry, but Professor Hoskins has shown that this is a myth, and that none of them came to Devon before the 12th century.[61]

John was the second son of Christopher Copleston of Warleigh, High Sherrif of Devon in 1561, who killed Christopher Monnes (said to be his godson) in a quarrel by the Copleston Oak tree on Tamerton village green. After appealing to the Queen, Christopher was granted a pardon for the crime, and on his death in 1589 he was buried in the vault in this church.[62]

There is another Copleston monument, on the south wall of the north aisle, and this is in memory of Susannah the daughter of the above-mentioned John. In 1615 she married Edward Calmady, the brother of Sir Shilston Calmady of Leewood near Bridestowe, and she died in 1617. The ladies at her sides are probably two of her sisters, Phillipa who married Sir Nicholas Slanning of Maristow, and Joan who married William Crymes of Buckland Monachorum.

Beneath the above monument is one to a young boy, Copleston Bampfylde second son of Sir Copleston Bampfylde of Poltimore and Warleigh. The long inscription in Latin and Greek[63] tells us that he was ten years old when he died in 1669, and that he was something of a paragon:—

"Renowned for the purity of his life,
In the excellence of his appearance,
the grace of his manners,
Second to none.
Studious beyond his years
Fortunate in his progress
Excelling in both respects.
Especially exalted in his very nature, but
Outstanding in his complete humility . . ."

John and Susannah Copleston
and their family.

The eagle displayed
(centre) shows the link
with the Rous family.

Copleston Bampfylde
the boy of
prodigious learning.

Radcliffe
memorial
hatchments.

A nearby floorstone commemorates another member of this family, namely Margaret the daughter of Hugh Bampfylde. She died in 1686, and the wording on the stone says:—

"Her make was too refined for this gross sphere."

An adjacent floorstone names seven members of the Radcliffe family who died between 1745 and 1817. The family purchased the manors of Warleigh and Tamerton and moved to the Warleigh estate in 1741; the descendants from this family still live here, their predecessors being commemorated by a series of memorial tablets on the north wall behind the family pew. There are also two memorial hatchments above the arches in the north aisle: the first commemorates the death in 1752 of the first Walter Radcliffe to own Warleigh, whilst the other commemorates his second son who died in 1803. Both will have been displayed initially at the entrance to Warleigh House, and later moved to the church.

Outside the choir vestry two floorstones relate to Samuel Madock of Plymouth, a merchant who died in 1713, his wife the Hon. Isabella daughter of Lord Mohun, and their two children Catherine and James.

Nathaniel Howard, a poet and Persian scholar, has a memorial on the north wall, although he was not buried here. He lived at Harwood House in the village from 1811 to 1828, and ran a boarding school there, teaching the boys the classical languages as well as English and Mathematics.[64] The grave of his son, the Rev. Nathaniel Arscott Howard, is in the churchyard.

On the south wall is a memorial to a former churchwarden, Richard Bold and his wife Anne, both of whom died in 1776. Their daughter says rather sadly:

". . . cruel death hath stopped their breath
And left me here to moan."

John Brown, a gardener and nurseryman and former churchwarden, who died in 1852, is commemorated for his bequest of money to purchase 12 pairs of men's shoes every year, "to be given to 12 honest labourers of the parish".

The Rev. John Rayner, who died aged 28 in 1829 having been Vicar for only two years, has a tablet "erected by the poor of the place, commemorative of his qualities as their pastor".

Not to be outdone by the efforts in verse within the church, a farmer called William Reep who died in 1792, and seems to have been the village stonemason, is commemorated in the churchyard by a poetic epitaph on his gravestone clearly intended that he should not be easily forgotten:

"He who inscribed the monumental tale
How lived how died the Tenants of the vale
. . .   . . .
Shall HE unnoticed sink into the grave
And want the Tablet he to others gave?
Forbid it Justice, here consigned to sleep
Should be unnoticed, Farmer William Reep."

The adjacent stone relates to his son, Gus Reep, who died aged eight, and also his daughter Elizabeth Reep. On the reverse side of this stone appears the words:

"Unhappy Day in Killing CHARLES our KING
More Grief than Joy, CHILDREN to PARENTS bring."

A strange inscription since Charles I was beheaded over a century earlier, on 30th January 1649; Gus Reep was born on the same date in 1758. William Reep must have had strong royalist sympathies. There is no reference to Mrs. Reep's burial, perhaps she wrote the verses, and had no-one left to sing her praises.

The earliest identifiable gravestone is that of William Oliver who died in 1735; another attractively decorated one is that to William Hearn, died 1766.

The Church Bells

We know from the inventory prepared by Edward VI's Commissioners that in the year 1553 Tamerton Foliot church had four bells in the tower, although a number of other churches in the district had no more than three. There is no record of the name of the original bell founder, but it is possible that the Tamerton bells came from the foundry at Exeter which was casting about the time that the nave and tower were built (1440-1450). A Terrier (or church inventory) drawn up in 1727 confirms the existence then of the four bells.

In the second half of the 18th century John Pennington of Lezant was travelling round East Cornwall and West Devon casting bells for churches and he made a visit to Tamerton Foliot. Perhaps the old bells there had gone out of tune, or developed cracks; or maybe they were concerned at the growing fashion for other churches in the area to add to their peals. At all events it was decided to recast the four bells here and to add two trebles to make a peal of six, and in 1773 Pennington was paid £111 for the work.[65] It is a pity that in the recasting the identity marks of the original founder were lost. Pennington had dug his casting moulds in pits on the village green, and when he sought to re-use the same pits to cast bells for another church permission was refused by the lord of the manor who ordered him to fill them in.[66]

The 18th century church accounts show that the bell ropes were being replaced every two or three years and the old ropes sold. It is of interest to note that the average life of the ropes used today is closer to seven years. The bells themselves were rehung in 1880 by Mr. Aggett a Church Bell Hanger from Chagford; and again in 1936 by the firm of Gillett and Johnson who rehung them on an H-type frame and also retuned them. After the latter event they were rededicated.

In 1902 a box of 19 handbells was presented to the church. In 1972 the ringing chamber was glassed in with a screen erected in memory of the previous vicar, A. R. Leggate.

St. Mary's Church has often had visiting teams to ring the changes on its bells, and its own ringers have competed successfully in ringing competitions in churches throughout the district, an activity which involves the closest co-operation between the captain of the ringers and his team. A report that survives from early this century suggests that such close harmony has not always prevailed:

"*The captain would not ring, but would have the old-fashioned chiming, so a dispute arose and the ringers had to see the churchwarden who considered that ringing instead of chiming was an improvement.*"

It is to be hoped that they settled it amicably! Chiming is when the clapper strikes the motionless bell; ringing means that the bell swings freely, producing a different tone.

Organ

The organ was built by Hele & Co. of Plymouth, and installed in 1895. It is two-manual, and is fitted with a Royal College of Organists pedal board. The organ was restored by George Osmond of Taunton in 1936, and a Gamba put in on the swell; they added a balanced swell pedal in 1980, and are responsible for the regular maintenance of the instrument.

The Church Plate

The Church possesses several pieces of valuable silver. The three oldest and finest are now deposited for safe keeping in the Buckland Abbey Museum. These are an Elizabethan Communion Cup with its cover (in the shape of a Paten, or plate) dated 1576, very attractively ornamented and bearing an Exeter goldsmith's mark;[67] also a fine tankard Flagon for the Communion wine, dated 1722; and a large Paten (or plate, for the bread or wafers) date 1717. The Exeter goldsmiths did not have the statutory authority before 1700 to make an assay mark on plate, and the 1576 Communion Cup was probably marked during the period of anti-popery, when there was a demand for medieval chalices to be melted down and reshaped into deeper cups as required by the Protestant Reformers, who insisted that the congregation should receive their communion in both bread and wine.

There is also a modern Chalice together with a Paten, dated 1945, and a Wafer Box 1944, which are at present in use in the Church.

Pulpit

The pulpit is an interesting and attractive example of carved woodwork in oak, and unusual in having nine panels. It has been made up from pieces worked in different styles, the main framing being Jacobean. The small panels round the top, bearing a winged cherub and other types of ornamentation, are renaissance work, whilst the inset panels below are Tudor linenfold. The bottom panels with the inscription date from about 1700, but the base and the steps are late 19th century work.

Throughout the 18th and the first half of the 19th century the pulpit stood in the middle of the nave, near the east end, completely blocking the view of the communion table and so emphasising the importance placed on preaching, since at that time it was customary to take communion only three times in the year. The pulpit was reached by a flight of wooden steps, and below it was the reading desk in a small pew for the clerk. Suspended above the pulpit was a rather handsome canopy in oak, bearing on the panels round its sides an inscription from Romans X, v.14: "How shall they believe in Him of whom they have not heard? How shall they hear without a preacher?"[68]

In 1851 the pulpit was moved to the north side of the nave, opening up the view of the altar. Possibly the canopy was damaged in the move, and the inscribed panels were salvaged and fitted round the base of the pulpit where they can now be seen more easily.

Font

The octagonal font is of moorstone, Perpendicular in style, probably 15th century, and it bears small shields on the sides and trefoiled panels on the column.

It has not always been in its present position. An early 19th century plan shows it at the east end of the north aisle, whilst a slightly later plan placed it at the back of the nave in front of the tower, and the Rural Dean's report of 1834 stated: "It has been judiciously moved to give more room for children under the west gallery." By 1890 however it was transferred to its present position at the back of the south aisle, and in 1896 a brass font ewer was presented to the church "by the children of the parish."[69]

The roof bosses

The roof in St. Mary's Church is a wagon or barrel type which is common to many churches in south west Devon. When first built it may have been open to the rafters, but at some later stage a plaster ceiling was added presumably to make the building warmer.

On the underside of the ceiling is what can justifiably be called the hidden treasure of the church, namely its roof bosses, which are perhaps hardly noticed by congregation or casual visitor, and are certainly never fully appreciated because they cannot be seen properly. Appropriate artificial illumination would remedy this.

The series of carved wooden roof bosses, probably because of their inaccessibility, escaped destruction during the waves of puritan vandalism. Polwhele's "History of Devonshire", written about 1796, states that the Tamerton bosses were ornamented with the armorial bearings of the manorial families of Gorges, Foliots, and Copleston, but it is difficult to identify any of these today and it is known that some were damaged irreparably during the 19th century building restorations; a few such were later replaced by plaster casts.

The bosses in the nave and south aisle, thought to be of 15th century origin, are circular, and a number of them bear the curious motif of a face or head with leafy stems growing out of the mouth, the symbolism of which may be connected with pre-Christian tree-worship or desire for the success of the harvest.[70] Others seem to be foliage designs, and some resemble whirls like whipped cream suggestive of the whirlpool in the Gorges arms. The bosses in the north aisle are smaller, square in shape, and could be of an earlier date; they include carved portrayals of a medieval tunic, blacksmith's tools, a Tudor rose and also various leaf designs.

Similar bosses of both types occur in other churches in the south west, which suggests that they may have been carved in a central workshop or by a group of travelling wood-carvers.

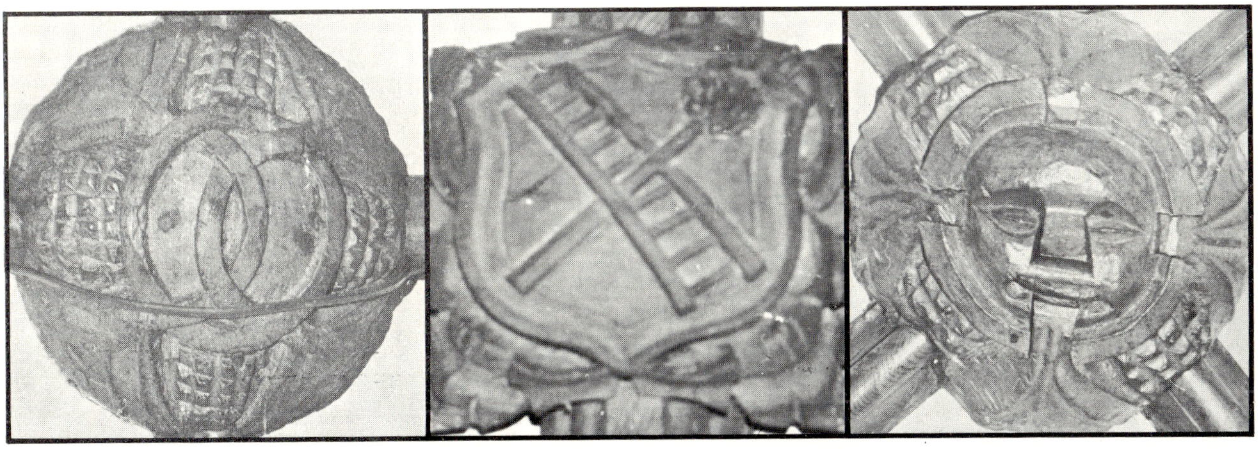

The disastrous fire which destroyed the roof of the nave and much of the roof of the north aisle on the 18th September 1981 miraculously did not seriously damage any of the bosses; even torrential rain and high winds on the following day failed to dislodge a single one. It was as if the hand of Providence had protected them.

Church and Community

The Parish system, which was started as far back as Saxon times, has been a unit of both ecclesiastical and civil government.[71] The election of the churchwardens dates back to the 13th century, and together with the other members of the Parish Vestry Committee they became an important part of local government under the Tudors, at the time when the powers of the medieval manors were declining. Under Elizabeth I the churchwardens became in effect ecclesiastical magistrates in their parishes,[72] levying rates on local property-owners for the maintenance of the church building and also the parish highways, as well as for the relief of the poor. They continued to do this until late in the 19th century, when the power to levy rates was taken from them by the government, and given to the newly-established secular bodies such as the County and Parish Councils.

The earliest surviving Tamerton Vestry record relates to Poor Relief and dates back to 1730, in which year the churchwardens levied a Poor Rate of sixpence in the £ on all local estates and houses, raising a total of £47 for the year, and of this £28 was expended. The record provides us with the earliest complete list of houses and farms in the parish and their owners. Poor Relief granted in kind included firewood, blankets, shoes and clothing; relief in cash varied from four shillings (20p) to nine shillings (45p) a month, according to the Vestry Committee's view of the need. Payment was made for a lad to be an indentured apprentice. In 1734 the Committee paid the following funeral expenses:—

Coffin for Robert Downing	10s 0d	(50p)
Liquor at his funeral	2s 6d	(12½p)
For woll (the woollen shroud)	8d	(3p)
Minister	2s 6d	
Affidavit (Death Certificate)	1s 0d	(5p)
Laying forth and Watching 3 nights	6s 4d	(32p)
Digging the grave	1s 6d	(7½p)
	£1.4s 6d	

The Vestry Committee did not show over-much sympathy with the parish poor when in 1820 they decided that "All who receive Parish Relief shall be distinguished by the letters T P (Tamerton Poor) on some conspicuous part of their dress, except only for the aged and infirm."[73] Concerned that illegitimate children too often became a charge upon the local ratepayers they resolved "That Lieut. Huskisson and Capt. Bevan Redward be compelled to indemnify the Parish for their base children." The same Committee considered that a labourer earning nine shillings a week and living rent free, should (except in case of his own sickness) be able to maintain himself, his wife and three children. It is not surprising to learn that the members were all property-owners.

There were individuals however who were anxious about the problems of poverty. In 1669 Dame Gertrude Bampfylde's Will provided four cottages (the "Gift Houses") for the accommodation of four poor widows from the parish; and a number of charitable trusts were set up by individuals during the 19th century, for the relief of the poor, usually naming the vicar and churchwardens amongst the trustees. In 1826 the Bampfylde almshouse in Horsham Lane, was built on land provided by Mr. Radcliffe the lord of the manor; it opened with a master and 16 occupants. By 1834 responsibility for Poor Relief was taken out of the hands of the Vestry, and transferred to a Board of Guardians; this proved little more than a change of name, since the same individuals were appointed Overseers of the Poor and they took over the financing and distribution of relief. It is interesting to note that in 1851 on the appointment of the village policeman, the cost of his clothing and wages was charged against the income from the Poor Rates.[74]

Mary Dean's Charity School, established in 1734, was from the beginning to be closely linked with the village church. Mrs. Dean had laid down that the teaching in the school should include "the Church of England catechism and the principles of the Christian religion". Prayers were to be said in the school daily, and the master was to take the boys to church every Sunday and Holy Day, seating being allotted to them at the back. The early records however make no reference to the school other than its regular assessments for payment of rates. On the passing of the 1870 Education Act which was to make education available to all children, the Vestry Committee sprang into action, apparently fearful that the government would impose on the parish a school over which they would have little control, and for which they might have to pay a new and heavy education rate. To avoid this they decided to set up their own Voluntary School, and elected a School Board to establish and manage it. A new school, with a house for the master and the mistress, was built on a site on Rock Hill given by Mr. Radcliffe, the lord of the manor, and the old school house on Fore Street (now a private house called 'Hillside') was sold.

The cost of the building was largely met out of the funds of the Mary Dean Charity. The first Governing Body of the School was set up in 1874, and included three people elected by the Vestry Committee, the Vicar being an ex-officio member, so from this date the Church of St. Mary became formally involved in education in the parish other than the provision of a Sunday School in the old Warleigh Room. Although the provision of public education has since then been taken over by the Local Education Authority (now Devon County Council) and Mary Dean's School moved in 1976 to new and larger premises in Jessop's Park, it has remained a Voluntary Controlled School, closely associated with our village church, the Vicar being chairman of the School Governors.

The churchwardens' account books show that in 1775 new village stocks were purchased, and these were still in use in 1821 when a new lock for them was purchased; these same stocks are now to be found in the entrance porch to the church. Security was a problem in those days, and in 1805 notices were printed and advertisements published in the Exeter and the Sherborne papers concerning a robbery in St. Mary's Church; it is perhaps not very surprising that soon afterwards they bought a new iron chest for the safe keeping of the church papers and plate.[75]

The same accounts include, until about 1840, payments made by the churchwardens for the destruction of pests considered detrimental to parish crops or stock; thus any boy who handed in a fox's or a badger's head in 1774 was paid one shilling; in 1784 hoop heads (bullfinches) were rewarded at a penny each, and in 1833 over 120 of these birds were so destroyed. By this latter date the growing of fruit trees had become an important part of the livelihood of people in and around the village. A somewhat different item was represented by the sum of £12 paid in 1855 to a mason for cutting a flight of steps in the granite rock, to provide easier access to the churchyard from Church Row Lane; since the average wage then being paid to a skilled labourer was 8/- per week, this sum covered about 30 weeks work. At the same time the parishioners were being made aware of their missionary responsibility, and in 1852 a "Collection for preaching the Gospel to the Irish in their native tongue" raised a total of £4 15s 3½d,[76] small repayment it would seem for the visit by St. Indract 1,000 years before!

The state of the parish roads was always a problem. The churchwardens nominated an individual, usually a member of the Vestry Committee, to act as Surveyor of the Highway. He would hire farm carts to fetch stones from barges on the creek or from one of the local quarries, and pay labourers to spread the stones on the roads so as to fill up the holes. Not surprisingly this was never a very satisfactory method of repair. Owners of private carriages frequently complained, and John Brown the Surveyor from 1846 to 1848 recorded that the owner of Uplands on Looseleigh Lane wanted to have "the part of the road he travels over, namely from his entrance gate to the Turnpike kept in such a manner that it would have incurred a very considerable expense". The Turnpike road was the main road from Plymouth to Tavistock. Brown, who was a nurseryman in the village, had previously been a Guardian of the Poor and he was a Churchwarden from 1838 to 1852.

Numerous other local problems came before the Vestry Committee, and during the second half of the 19th century the members were much concerned to improve the village water supply and provide more efficient disposal of sewage. In 1893 they made a successful application for the Postal Authorities to open a telegraph delivery office in the village.

The Tamerton village green (sometimes referred to as Cann Green), the scene of all kinds of open-air social gatherings, was on a piece of ground at the eastern end of the church. Here for six centuries flourished the annual July Horn Fair, as well as the autumn market on the Feast of St. Denis[77] (9th October); but both were gradually supplanted by larger functions in nearby towns, and by 1870 both had ceased to exist. The lord of the manor, as owner of the green, then donated part of it for an extension to the churchyard, leaving only the small triangle of land on which stands the Copleston oak tree;[78] in 1979 Mr. Radcliffe gave this remaining portion to Plymouth Corporation.

The churchyard provides for the needs of the whole parish, whether members of this church or not; thus not only has it been necessary to extend it three times, but also from time to time older parts of the burial ground have been re-used. Over the centuries churches have often had to do this, and it may explain why the ground on the south side of Tamerton Foliot church is a foot or two higher than the adjacent pathway and the church floor. The northern part of the churchyard adjoining the church, is now reserved for cremated remains, and the cost of removing and resiting the headstones affected was met by a bequest from a relative of the then Vicar. There is a memorial stone commemorating this, in the centre of that area, and also a memorial book in the north aisle of the church.

After the 1939-1945 war a large new Council housing estate was built in the Southway district of the parish, resulting in a dramatic increase in its population and the need for a church to serve that area. A site was allocated, and with monies received from war-damage claims the Diocese erected a church-cum-hall, the Church of the Holy Spirit, which was dedicated on Whitsunday, the 4th of June 1960. The original intention had been to share its use with other denominations, and although relations with them are good they have preferred to use their own premises. Southway was designated as a separate parish in 1971, reducing the area of the original Tamerton parish by about a quarter.

The Church Hall was opened in 1974, the fulfilment of a century-old dream by people in the parish. Built at a cost of £23,000 it was paid for in a remarkably short time, principally out of various grants supplemented by a series of loans from parishioners which were repaid from income arising out of hiring the hall. It has provided a focal centre for village activities and been extensively used by the whole community. The Hall replaced a wooden hut which had been used since 1922 and was burnt down, and also the old Warleigh Room. The latter was an 18th century building, owned by the lord of the manor and used mainly for church activities. For many years it housed the Sunday School classes, and occasionally it provided extra accommodation for Mary Dean's school and was commonly referred to as "the old schoolroom"; latterly it had also been used for meetings of the Parochial Church Council (the modern Vestry Committee). Its limited size, lack of facilities and poor state of repair left little alternative to its replacement.

Tamerton Charities

In addition to Mary Dean's Endowed School, eleven other charitable foundations were established in the parish over the past 300 years, all concerned with giving assistance to the deserving poor, in some cases in money, in others as bread or clothing. The earliest was the Dame Gertrude Bampfylde bequest under her Will of 1669 which set up the "Gift Houses" in Church Row Lane for the accommodation of four poor widows; a subsequent charity left money to provide the widows with an annual income. Others provided:—

"*Warm winter clothing to aged poor women of the parish.*"

"*Coals and wood, to be distributed amongst twelve sober, honest and industrious poor.*"

"*Blankets to those in need.*"

"*Twelve pairs of men's good strong working shoes, nailed and fitted in the manner in which poor agricultural labourers usually wear them, each recipient to be resident in the parish at least three years and to have at least two children all maintained chiefly by his honest exertions.*"

Fines inposed for unlawfully racing animals on Roborough Down in the parish in 1791 and again in 1825, were added to one endowment which was intended to provide clothing, so that the benefits from this charity became popularly known as "horse-racing petticoats".

One scheme provided pensions for former workers on the Maristow estate. Before the National Health Service was established another parish charity provided free treatment for poor parishioners at the Eye Infirmary or in one of the local hospitals.

The eleven charities are now all amalgamated into one fund known as the Parish United Charities Scheme, the income of which is used either to make grants of money or to pay for items or services calculated to reduce need, hardship or distress. The scheme is administered by five trustees of which the Vicar is one.

Reference Sources

Ref. no.

1 Plymouth, A New History, by Crispin Gill, Vol.I, p.19. Hoskins' 'Devon' states that Exeter was their western frontier town (p.36).

2 The Place-Names of Devon, by Gover, Mawer & Stenton, Part I, p.xvii.

3 History and Imagery in British Churches, by Anderson, p.34.

4 Devon, by Hoskins, p.222.

5. Lives of St. Indract and St. Dominic, by Doble, p.4. Baring-Gould considered that Indract was not Irish but was the abbot of Iona. (J.R.I.C., Vol.14, p.279)

6 Doble, p.22. Coulson's "Biographical Dictionary of the Saints" however quotes February 5th. Crispin Gill (p.25) says that Tamerton Foliot church was dedicated to St. Indract, until its re-dedication to St. Mary in 1318.

7 Plymouth, A New History, Vol.I, p.28.

8 The Churches of Devon, by Slader, p.24.

9 History and Imagery in British Churches, p.37.

10 The Devonshire Domesday, pub. Devonshire Association, p.1045.

11 Exeter Diocesan papers in Devon Record Office, ref.ED/PP/8.

12 Taxatio Ecclesiastica of Pope Nicholas, 1291.

13 Devon, by Hoskins, p.225.

14 The Hundreds of Devon, by Reichel, p.122, quoting the Calendar of Papal Regs., I, 549. The Feast of St. Denis was on 9th October.

15 Article by Hamilton Thompson in the Archaeological Journal for 1913. The dedication was on the octave of the Feast of the Assumption of the Blessed Virgin Mary (22 August).

16 Two articles by J. C. Bellamy in the Plymouth, Devonport and Stonehouse Herald 1853. Bellamy had seen the church before any of the 1851-52 rebuilding took place. Miss B. Cresswell in her MSS Notes on Devon Churches (1911, revised 1922) considered that the 14th century Tamerton church was cruciform in shape, but I can find no evidence to support this.

17 Devon, by Hoskins, pp.170 and 271.

18 Sir William Glynne's Notes on the Churches of Devon, p.78 (in the West Country Studies Library, Exeter). He visited Tamerton Foliot in 1852.

19 See plan of church in early 19th century, Rad.MSS.407/4/XYZ(1) West Devon Record Office, Plymouth.

20 Medieval Panorama, by G. C. Coulton, p.496.

21 Devon, by Hoskins, p.227.

22 Devon and Cornwall Notes & Queries, Vol.14/95.

23 Monasticon Diocesis Exoniensis, by Oliver, p.480.

24 Devon, p.232.

25 Plympton Erle, by Brookings Rowe, p.239.

26 The Rings of Church Bells in the City of Plymouth, pamphlet by F. S. Worth, pub.1953, quoting from 'The Church Bells of St. Budeaux' by Rev. T. A. Hancock.

27 The Act of Uniformity 1552.

28 Bellamy, Newspaper Articles (quoted above), 1853.

29 Sir William Glynne's Notes on Devon Churches.

30 Devon, p.238.

31 Parish Churches of England, by Cox & Ford, p.14.

32 Churchwardens' Accounts, annually 1833-1849.

33 Churchwardens' Accounts 1811.

34 The Acts of 1643 and 1644 "abolishing supersitious monuments in Churches, including organs".

35 Churchwardens' Accounts 1783.

36 Rural Dean's Report 1854.

37 Abstract of Accounts for repairs and alterations to Tamerton Foliot Church, July 1850, Rad.MSS. 407/4/XYZ(1).

38 Churchwardens' Accounts and Poor Rate Books, 1850-1852.

39 Rad.MSS. 407/4/XYZ(1) and (2). Part of the old woodwork was re-used in the alterations to the pews, but the numbers on the pew doors were not kept in consecutive order and still remain so today, some being missing.

40 Poor Rate Book 1850 and Rad.MSS. 407/4/XYZ(2).

41 Rural Dean's Report 1865.

42 Vestry Committee Minutes March 1885 and June 1891.

43 Vestry Minutes June 1891 and Rural Dean's Report 1885.

44 These traces were visible in 1852 according to Bellamy.

45 Vestry Minutes 9 April 1901.

46 Rural Dean's Reports, 1887, 1890, 1896.
47 Churchwardens' Accounts 1849-1896.
48 Rad.MSS. 407/4/XYZ(2).
49 Rural Dean's Report 1896.
50 Vestry Minutes 11 April 1912.
51 Exeter Episcopal Registers 1257-1307, p.183.
52 ED/PP/13 (1291), D.R.O. Exeter.
53 Valor Ecclesiasticus (26 Henry VIII, 1535).
54 Calendar of the Archives of Exeter Cathedral, 1873.
55 Moget File, Vol.2, D.R.O. Exeter: see frontispiece illustration.
56 Worth's Dartmoor, p.409.
57 Tamerton Foliot Tithe Map, 1840 (D.R.O. Exeter).
58 Bishop of Exeter's consent to the building of a new Vicarage in a letter dated 27 April 1775, W.D.R.O. Plymouth.
59 Gilbert Foliot and his letters, by Morey & Brooke, p.35.
60 Rad.MSS. 407/4/XYZ(1).
61 Devon, by Hoskins, p.76.
62 Note on the Copleston monuments, by W. N. Radcliffe.
63 At the foot of the monument.
64 Rowe's Plymouth Directory for 1814.
65 Rad.MSS. 407/4/XYZ(2).
66 Rad.MSS. 407/8/L3.
67 Exeter Catalogue of Silver, pp.3 and 4. John Jones, whose mark appears on the Plymouth (Tamerton Foliot) plate converted about 130 chalices in the Exeter diocese.
68 Notes on Tamerton Foliot Church, by Davidson, 1840. Also newspaper articles by Bellamy, 1853.
69 Rural Dean's Report 1896.
70 Roof Bosses in Medieval Churches, by Cave, p.16.
71 Plymouth, A New History, Vol.I, by Crispin Gill, p.28. Also: Sources for English Local History, by W. B. Stephens, p.44.
72 Parish Churches of England, by Cox & Ford, p.20.
73 Vestry Minutes 5 January 1820.
74 Poor Rates Book 20 February 1852.
75 Churchwardens' Accounts 1813.
76 Poor Rates Book 23 May 1852.
77 The Feast of St. Denis is 9th October, and the choice of this date seems to have been accidental; there is no obvious reason for Tamerton honouring the patron saint of France. The right to hold a market and also annual fairs in the village was granted by Henry III in 1270 (repeated by Edward I in 1293) — see First Report of Royal Commission on Market Rights and Tolls, 1889.
78 Vestry Minutes April/May 1870. Also Rural Dean's Report 1871.

Calendar of Events

About 689 AD	St. Indract begins converting Tamerunta; it is possible that he founded the first church here.
Since c.900	Existence of regular Christian worship here, possibly earlier than this date.
1086	Domesday Survey records no mention of a church here.
1250	Warleigh House chapel licensed by the Bishop.
1270	Tamerton Foliot granted the right by Henry III to hold a weekly market and twice-yearly fairs.
1279	Sir Richard le Deneis given the custody of Tamerton Foliot Vicarage by Bishop Bronescombe.
1288	Papal Valuation made of church property; Tamerton Foliot valued at £4.
1292	Tamerton Foliot held Borough status.
1292	Church here in process of alteration.
1318	High Altar and three other altars dedicated by the Bishop, in the church of St. Mary the Virgin, Tamerton Foliot.
1343	The right granted to the Tamerton Foliot burgesses to choose their own Reeve, and hold manorial courts in the Borough.
1346	Supposed date of the oldest monument in the church (the Gorges tomb; its existence confirmed here in 1350).
14th century	People preached to in their own language. Few seats.
1410	Bishop Stafford provided money for the repair of bridges and roads in this area.
c.1440	Wide nave and chancel added to the church, and tower built.
c.1530	South aisle added.
c.1500	Chantry endowed in Tamerton church (Suppressed c.1560).
16th century	Lord of the manor had his own pew in the church.
1529	Reformation, and Henry VIII's break with the Pope.
1535	Vicarage and benefice valued at £10 in the General Ecclesiastical Survey of Henry VIII.
1536	Patronage of Tamerton Foliot church transferred from the Convent at Plympton to the King.
1552	The Act of Uniformity imposed a duty on all persons to attend divine service on every Sunday and Holy Day, unless they had "a lawful or reasonable excuse to be absent."
1553	Commissioners' Inventory records four bells in the tower.
1576	Date marked on the Elizabethan Communion Chalice.
1583	Impropriate (lay) Rectorship first granted by Elizabeth I.
1562	John Copleston of Warleigh killed his godson Christopher Monnes by the Copleston Oak on the village green on 22 March; later that year he was granted an official pardon for the manslaughter.
1601	Earliest surviving Terrier (Inventory) for the church and glebe at Tamerton Foliot.
1613	A further Terrier, adding details about the Vicarage.
1617	Copleston Memorial erected.
1644	Cromwell and orders about music in church.
1669	Copleston Bampfylde Memorial.
1669	The Gift Houses provided through a legacy from Dame Gertrude Bampfylde.
1717	Holy Communion paten dated.
1722	Holy Communion flagon dated.
1727	First mention of a tower clock.
1734	Mary Dean's Charity School officially established, at a house in the village.
1741	Radcliffe family acquire Warleigh and the manor of Tamerton Foliot.
1745	Church Terrier lists a Vicarage, orchard and herb garden.
18th century	Regular expenditure on new fiddle strings for the church orchestra. Bell ropes replaced every two or three years. Pulpit stands in the middle of the nave.
1773	Church bells recast and increased from four to six.
1775-1776	Vicarage rebuilt (the present building).
1775	New stocks purchased (now in the church porch).
1794	Early church registers destroyed by fire, apparently after removal from the church.
1805	New iron chest purchased for safe keeping of church papers and silver plate.
1811	Wooden gallery added to back of south aisle.
1820	Letters T P (Tamerton Poor) ordered to be attached to the dress of certain people receiving parish charity.

1821	New lock purchased for the stocks.
1823	Rural Dean criticises outside drainage of the church.
1825	Archdeacon criticises disproportionately large amount of rented pew-space, and the ignoring of his instructions to provide more seating for the poor.
1826	Bampfylde almshouse built in Horsham Lane.
1834	Responsibility for poor relief transferred from the Vestry to the new Board of Guardians.
1836	First Act of Parliament to eliminate tithes.
1846	Harmonium obtained by the church.
1849	Striking mechanism added to the church clock.
1850	A writer records: "No stained glass windows in this church, nor any cross on the altar."
1851	Major repairs to the south aisle and porch: £700 raised. Galleries taken down and replaced by a new one at rear of nave; church floor raised two feet; pulpit moved to north side of nave.
1852	Old high box pews cut down and altered to present-day form.
1850-1900	Village water supply and sewerage disposal gradually improved.
1868	Radcliffe Memorial Window inserted at the east end, over the altar — the first stained glass window to be put in the church since the Reformation.
1870	Churchyard extension, east end, taking in most of the old village green. (Since the annual July Horn Fair and the Autumn Market on the Feast of St. Denis — 9 October — had both ceased to exist.) An east wall with piers, gates and railings, erected to enclose the ground involved.
1877	New school buildings on Rock Hill for Mary Dean's School, to replace original premises on School Hill at the top of Fore Street.
1878	The old Tamerton Deanery abolished — it had existed since medieval times.
1880	Church bells rehung: cost £44.
1885	Brass lectern given by Sir Massey Lopes. Stained glass window put at west end of south aisle (Turner Macan).
1887	Western boundary wall to churchyard rebuilt with piers, iron gates and railings.
1888	Donation from Sir Massey Lopes permits removal of west gallery, erection of new carved screen at tower entrance, new flooring provided for the ringers, and the font removed to a Baptistry at the back of the south aisle.
1888-1891	Severe winter storms damage the north aisle roof.
1890	Stained glass window inserted in the south aisle (Griggs).
1893	Telegraph Delivery Office opened in the village.
1894	Additional ground given for an extension to the churchyard. The north aisle taken down and rebuilt five feet wider, its roof raised to match the rest of the church; the pulpit was repaired; new heating apparatus provided; a new altar table; and choir stalls provided. Total cost £2,000. The new Parish Councils took over all civil matters from the Vestry Committee.
1895	A pipe organ installed for £344; the cost of both this and last year's restoration of the building paid off by 1900. A stained glass window inserted in the south aisle (Lillicraps, Symons and Cornish).
1896	Brass font ewer presented by "the children of the parish".
1897	New tower clock presented by the Grigg family of Cann House.
1902	Brass alms dish donated. Box of handbells donated.
1905	Three windows re-glazed with Cathedral glass.
1909	Bells overhauled. Stained glass window inserted in west wall of tower (Copleston Lopes Radcliffe and his wife).
1910	Bathroom added to the Vicarage: cost £128.
1911	Proposal to replace existing seats with oak pews — never put into effect.
1914	East end of north aisle made into a Side Chapel, necessitating removal of Gorges tomb to present position. Oak reredos and panelling donated for the Sanctuary.
1922	Wooden hut erected near King's Arms PH, for use as a village hall.
1923	Electric lighting installed in the church and vicarage, supplied from a private generator in the village.
1926	Churchyard extended at west end.
1927	Vestry Committee opposes the proposed New Prayer Book.
1929	Church and vicarage connected to the mains electricity supply.

1930	Stained glass window put in west end of the north aisle (Pollexfen Colmore Copleson Radcliffe).
1933	Tower restoration: cost £398. Part of the glebe (vicarage garden) sold for a private house.
1935	New heating apparatus installed.
1935-1936	Death watch beetle found in tower; bell suspension replaced. First floor gallery provided for the ringers, enabling a choir vestry to be made on the ground floor of the tower.
1936	Tithes abolished by Act of Parliament.
1938	Organ renovated. Some evidence of beetle found in nave and south aisle.
1941	Air raid damages east window (repaired 1947-1948).
1954	Heating system overhauled and improved.
1956	New Inventory (Terrier) made of church property.
1950-1970	Southway Council Estate built.
1960	A new church built on Southway Estate, and dedicated to the Holy Spirit on Whitsunday 4th June 1960. St. Mary's heating system converted to gas firing.
1967	The tower clock overhauled and its faces repainted and refitted, the work done by John Smith of Derby.
1968	The church electric wiring and fittings renewed: cost £275. The village hut (the wooden hut) burnt down.
1970	The valuable old church silver plate transferred to Buckland Abbey Museum.
1971	The old parish registers and record books deposited in the West Devon Record Office, Tavistock Place, Plymouth. The Parish of Southway designated, reducing the size of Tamerton Foliot Parish.
1972	The Royal Coat of Arms restored by R. Morris, Dartington: £50. The bell ringing chamber glassed in (Leggate memorial). Part of the churchyard cleared and set aside for cremated remains; a Memorial Book maintained in the church to record these.
1974	The new Church Hall opened on 11 October 1974, on the site of the old Warleigh Room: cost £23,000.
1976	Mary Dean's school transferred from Rock Hill to a new building in Jessops Park. The Vicarage connected to the main drainage: cost £920. The Vicarage re-roofed.
1977	The Church re-slated: cost £7,000.
1979	The two small grassed areas east and west of the churchyard (by the War Memorial and by the Oak) given to Plymouth City Corporation by the Warleigh Estate.
1980	A swell pedal inserted in the organ.
1981	New guttering to the church roof. Three months later, late in the evening of 18th September, 1981, fire broke out in the roof of the nave above the altar, destroying most of the nave roof and much of the roof of the north aisle; torrential rain and high winds on the following day brought down much of the plaster ceiling of the nave. Although many of the wooden ribs were badly scorched, the roof bosses escaped serious damage, and the south aisle escaped altogether.

Records of the Church and Parish

The following records are now kept in the West Devon Record Office, in Plymouth:—
Church Registers from 1794 to 1897 (Baptisms), 1794 to 1948 (Marriages), 1794 to 1850 (Funerals).
Poor Rates Books 1728-1852
Surveyors of the Highways Book 1786-1810
Churchwardens' Account Books 1774-1953
Vestry Meetings (now called P.C.C.) 1818-1834 and 1866-1952.

The current records are in the hands of the Vicar, the Churchwardens and the Secretary to the Parochial Church Council.

The Royal Coat of Arms

As is the case in a number of other Anglican churches, the Royal Coat of Arms is displayed in this church where it is to be seen over the south porch as you leave the building. It was not always in this position; a writer in 1840 noted that it was fixed to the front of the west gallery, but the gallery was only in existence for about sixty years and was taken down in 1888. In what year the Arms were first put up here is not recorded, although churches did begin to display them after the Reformation apparently as a result of a local display of loyalty and not by any order from the sovereign or the government. They were taken down during the period of the Commonwealth (1649-1660) and put up again afterwards on the restoration of the monarchy, by order of Charles II.

The Coat of Arms which is now displayed in St. Mary's Church is that of H.M. William Frederick King George III, and has been identified as the Arms in use between 1801 and 1814. The three dates 1671, 1730 and 1810 which appear thereon are probably dates when the Arms were repainted and brought up to date with the details of the current sovereign; the two churchwardens named, Reverend Joseph Richards and Wm. Hull, were in office during the period 1809-1810. Subsequent restorers of the painting made no attempt to revise the details. There is no compulsion to display the Arms, but they do provide us with a reminder that the Queen is the Supreme Governor of the Church of England, and might also signify that the right of patronage to the living of St. Mary's is vested in the Crown.

Stages in building this Church

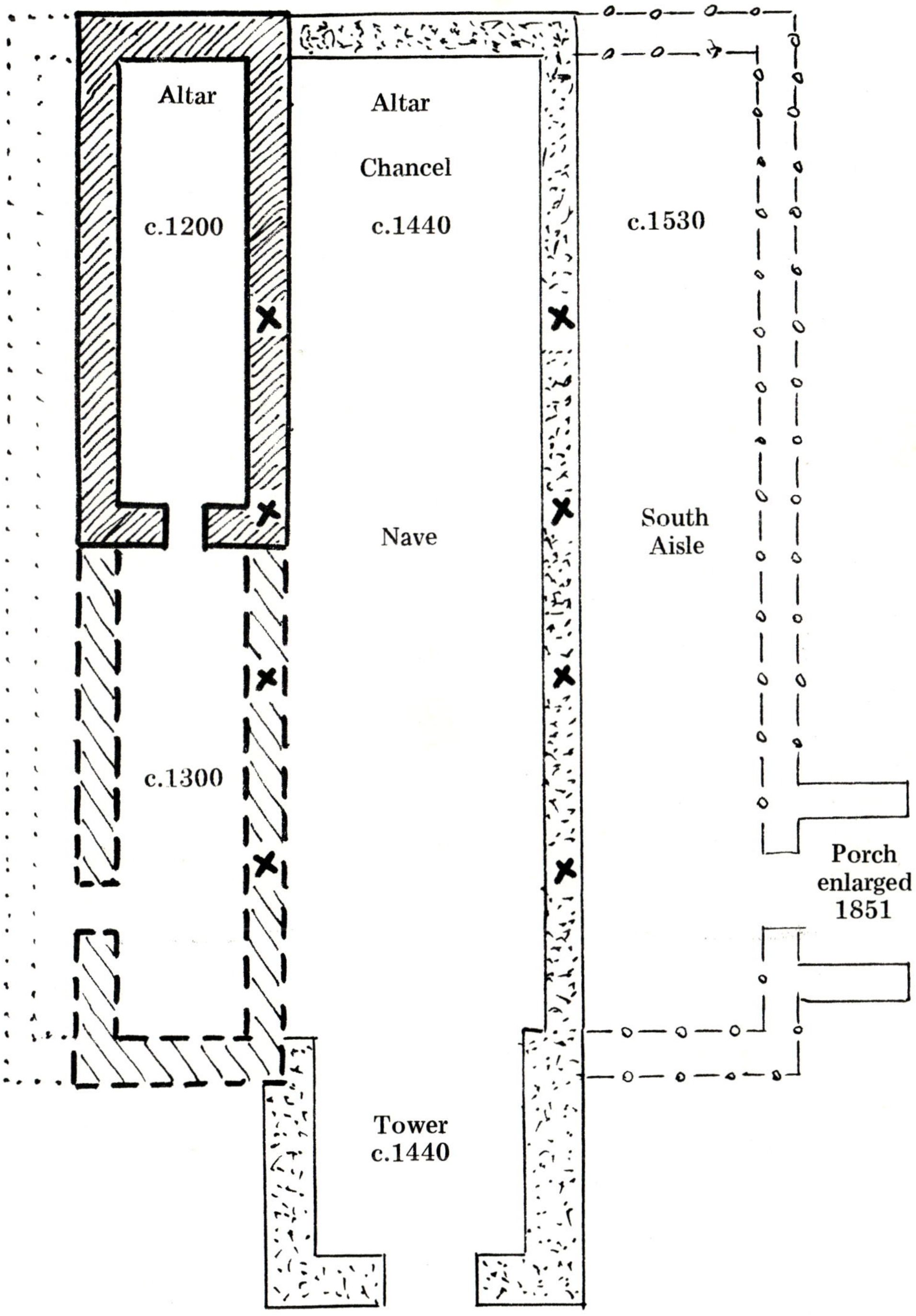

North aisle widened and rebuilt 1894-1895, roof raised to match rest of church.

South Aisle rebuilt 1851. Chancel and south aisle roofs raised to same level as nave roof.

The Church on Fire

Late in the evening of 18th September, 1981 a passing motor-cyclist noticed that the Church roof was on fire and gave the alarm. The Vicar's immediate reaction in spraying the altar and choir stalls with a fire extinguisher was successful in protecting them from burning embers falling from the roof. Thirty five firemen with six fire engines fought the blaze for several hours and brought it under control; their skill undoubtedly saved the building from complete destruction. Meanwhile many villagers braved the smoke and flames to rescue silver plate, vestments and other valuables. The roofs of both the nave and the north aisle were seriously damaged, but miraculously most of the contents of the Church were saved.